free Spirit
DOODLES

BY STEPHANIE CORFEE

CAPSTONE PRESS
a capstone imprint

Savvy Books are published by Capstone Press,
a Capstone imprint
1710 Roe Crest Drive
North Mankato, Minnesota 56003
www.mycapstone.com

Library of Congress Cataloging-in-Publication Data is
available at the Library of Congress website.

Summary: Be inspired to create one-of-a-kind masterpieces
that are earthy, breezy, and creative, and will help you
show off your carefree personality.

ISBN 978-1-4914-7945-2 (library binding);
ISBN 978-1-4914-7948-3 (ebook PDF)

Editor: Eliza Leahy
Designer: Lori Bye
Art Director: Heather Kindseth
The illustrations in this book were created with ink,
watercolors, and digitally.
Image Credits: Stephanie Corfee

Printed in China.
092015 009204S16S16

TABLE OF CONTENTS

ABOUT THIS BOOK

Doodling has so much to do with having a free spirit. The prettiest lines flow from your pen when you don't have a care in the world and just allow your mind to wander.

Sit outside. Get comfortable. Don't try to make everything perfect. When you begin to draw without any expectation of the outcome, your best work will shine through. It will be a true reflection of YOU!

Use this book as an inspiration to start a daily practice of doodling. Use it alongside a sketchbook of your own — or even blank pages from a notebook. Start out with ten minutes each day and see how far you can go toward expressing your true, free spirit!

5

Paint Pens
Opaque paint writes on practically anything with nice, vibrant color.

DOODLE TOOLS

You don't need anything fancy to doodle. A plain old pen and paper work just fine. But here are some fun tools to try that are definite winners!

Gel Pens
These create fine lines in a rainbow of colors! Keep white ones handy for adding doodles over darker colors.

Water Brushes
Water in the handle squeezes out to the brush! Perfect for adding watercolor effects to your permanent ink doodles — even on the go!

Mechanical Pencils
Always sharp, these draw like pens.
They're great for sketching outlines.

Pigment Ink Pens
A top pick for beautiful, detailed doodles
that are waterproof. You can find anything
from teeny point sizes to a juicy brush tip.

Ballpoint Pens
A great choice for doodling in
your school notebooks.

Markers
These are super for coloring
doodles since the color won't
cover your doodled lines.

TWIRLS & SWOOSHES

Get your wrist nice and loose by scribbling circles and loops.
Then practice the forms below, plus some of your own.

DOODLING PATTERNS

Building patterns with your doodles is so much fun. And you will amaze yourself with your creations. You can make coloring pages, greeting cards, or even wrapping paper that is one of a kind. The finished designs may look complex and impressive, but the process is amazingly simple. Patience is key. Create all-over patterns by scattering large doodles across the page. Then add medium-sized companion doodles in the spaces between them. Finally, finish the pattern by filling the remaining gaps with simple dots, sparkles, or other tiny accents. Striped patterns are built up in a similar way, with lines placed first, and then filled with doodles from largest to smallest. Once you master the process, pattern-making will be your new favorite way to spend an afternoon.

STEP-BY-STEP TOSSED PATTERNS

Create this sweet tossed pattern by drawing the elements step by step, starting with the designs in pink! Follow with green doodles and finally the purple. Add color if you like.

DECORATIVE NICKNAMES

Use pencil guides to create perfectly aligned nickname artworks.

Use light pencil to sketch in curves if you'd like to add some shape to your lettering. Here, do two upward waves, then divide the space based on the number of letters in each word. It's a great guide!

Write the words in the template you've made. Thick letters give you the most area for doodling, so be sure to keep your lettering nice and chunky.

LOVE BUG

Doodle and decorate each letter!
Follow the example shown here,
or create your own designs.

ADD COLOR!
Try colors that suit the
person with this nickname.

LOVELY LEAVES

Trace the outline of this tree branch onto a new sheet of paper. Then doodle designs on each leaf, trying not to repeat doodles. Challenge yourself!

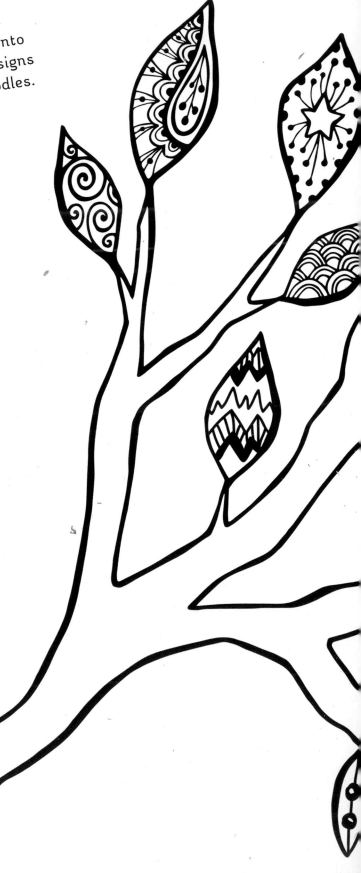

DREAM CATCHER

Make the circle form for your dream catcher, and draw a dot in the center. Add bows on each side and some beaded strings on the bottom.

Add several curved lines from the center of the circle to the frame. Thicken the bows and add some feathers, beads, and doodles.

Add more curved lines
from the center,
but bending in the
opposite direction.
This is key!
Complete with more
doodles on the frame
and feathers.

ADD COLOR!

Do you dream in color?
Close your eyes and
be inspired by the colors
in your dreams . . .
the many hues you can find
in sunsets, rainbows, and
fields of wildflowers.

MOONBEAM PENDANT

Doodle a magical pendant with your own wishing star.

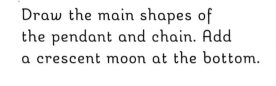

Draw the main shapes of
the pendant and chain. Add
a crescent moon at the bottom.

Expand the main shapes with
fancy scallops, swirls, petals,
dots, and the wishing star.

Continue to expand each shape and curve by adding more scallops, rows of dots, and thin lines, plus some tiny antenna-like bits for fun.

ADD COLOR!

Tell a story with the colors you choose by thinking of a color inspiration before you begin. Use the colors of a favorite place, a bouquet of flowers, or a favorite dress. Your finished art will hold extra-special meaning.

LOTUS LOVE

Symmetry and pattern combine in this zen-tastic blossom.

Draw four leaves that resemble a butterfly. Make two large ones and tuck two smaller ones beneath.

Layer leaf-shaped petals above the butterfly. The pale pink ones go first, then add the dark pink. Last, add an outline all around and a tiny cluster of petals at center.

Doodle in each petal and add long
swirls for extra delicate detail.

ADD COLOR!

Harmonious colors are used on each petal. Harmonious
colors are similar ones. For example, reds, pinks, and
oranges are harmonious. These color combos glow with
warmth and happiness.

MAKING SHAPES

Filling familiar shapes with your doodles is a cool way to create a strong theme. It makes sense, plus it is a lot of fun! Draw nature doodles inside a shape from nature, like a raindrop or feather. Draw groovy doodles inside a groovy shape, like round sunglasses or a crescent moon.

A FULL HEART

Use this intricate doodle-filled heart shape to inspire your own doodle-filled shape on a clean sheet of paper. Try a doodle-filled heart, moon, or sunflower. Finish it off with color!

LOVE! LOVE! LOVE!

Try doodling the word "love" in three distinct styles. I've given you some floral inspiration below.

FIND INSPIRATION

Making your own coloring sheets can be all kinds of fun. Use these patterns for inspiration to create your own coloring sheets, or trace the doodles onto a clean sheet of paper and color them in however you like!

DOODLES TO COLOR!

Doodles are so excellent in black and white. But creating doodles to color is a pretty great idea. For one thing, coloring detailed designs is super relaxing and a great way to unwind. You will get lost in the process, and before you know it, you'll have a masterpiece! Create lots of shapes and spaces in these doodles for color. Fill an entire page! If you use permanent black ink for these drawings, you'll be able to use any medium to color — markers, watercolor, gel pens, colored pencils, and more.

Try creating the outline of a sugar skull, like the one below, and then fill it in with a variety of doodles to create the nose, eyes, and teeth. Add some decorative doodles too! If you have trouble making the outline, you can trace this one onto a new sheet of paper.

Tip:
Make copies of your black and white doodles before coloring so you can enjoy them again and again, and even share them with your friends!

PHOTO FABULOUS

School Memories

Doodle names and years on school pictures to make your memories super cute!

Doodling on your photos is so much fun. Grab some paint pens and get to work adding words, dates, and decorations!

Add Some Style

Doodle colorful and over-the-top decorations, accessories, and accents that are sure to bring a smile.

Draw some detail

Add a touch of magic with drawn-on whimsical elements like wings, sparkles, and clouds to make sweet photos more like a fairy tale.

Share Your Emotions
Emojis aren't just for texting. These cute little guys tell it like it is.

Bon Voyage
Note the place and date in doodly style on your favorite vacation photos.

Fun Borders
Add rows of cute borders around any photo to give it an extra special touch. Use colors to match the photo and make it pop!

Lovefest
Doodled hearts on photos are a classic. Bonus points for a heart-shaped photo cut-out.

Best Friends Forever

SISTERS = xoxo BEST FRIENDS

Add Some Silly!
Draw mustaches, glasses, funny eyebrows, rosy cheeks, and more to make your silly photos even sillier! These doodled snaps will make you laugh for years to come.

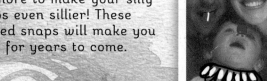

READ MORE

Bolte, Mari and Jennifer Rzasa. *Skater Chic Style: Fun Fashions You Can Sketch.* Drawing Fun Fashions. North Mankato, Minn.: Capstone Press, 2013.

Glaser, Byron and Sandra Higashi. *Zolocolor! Toodle-oo Doodle-oo.* New York: Little Simon, 2013.

Renouf, Eloise. *20 Ways to Draw a Tree and 44 Other Nifty Things from Nature: A Sketchbook for Artists, Designers, and Doodlers.* 20 Ways. Beverly, Mass.: Quarry Books, 2013.

INTERNET SITES

FactHound offers a safe, fun way to find Internet sites related to this book. All of the sites on FactHound have been researched by our staff.

Here's all you do:
Visit www.facthound.com
Type in this code: 9781491479452

ABOUT THE AUTHOR AND ILLUSTRATOR

Stephanie Corfee is an artist, designer, and author. She creates original and commissioned artworks combining paint and illustration, writes art books and kits, and licenses surface designs for gifts and accessories. She lives and works in Malvern, Pennsylvania.

Look for all the books in this series:

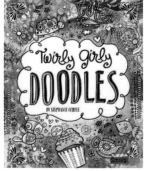
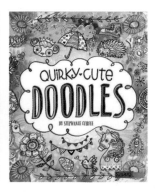